The Transformation Café

*7 Strategies to Help You Transform
From Who You Presently Are to
Who You Were Created to Be*

Joy Croel

Copyright © 2025 by Joy Croel

ISBN: 979-8-9928150-0-9

https://www.facebook.com/thetransformationcafe

All Rights Reserved. No part of this publication may be reproduced, distributed, or transmitted in any form or by any means, including photocopying, recording, or other electronic or mechanical methods, without the prior written permission of the publisher, except in the case of brief quotations embodied in critical reviews and certain other noncommercial uses permitted by copyright law.

For more information on purchases in bulk or speaking events, please contact the author at: JoyCroel@Gmail.com

Publishing Support Services by:
Motivational M.D. Enterprises www.imreadytolaunch.com

Table of Contents

Dedication 5
Acknowledgments..7
Foreword 9
Introduction 11
Chapter 1   Understand the Real Questions 15
Chapter 2   Know and Understand Your Purpose............... 21
Chapter 3   Learn to Believe In and Love Yourself 25
Chapter 4   Seek the One Resource That Will Change Your Life 29
Chapter 5   Understand, There's a Manual For This! 35
Chapter 6   Find Your Support Group 39
Chapter 7   Look For the Well 43
Closing Reflections.. 47
About the Author 49

Dedication

This book is dedicated to my sons: Leoris V. Jackson, L.V. Jackson, and Lannie F. Jackson; my daughter, Vanessa LaJoy Jackson; and my son, Jon David Croel, who learned by watching and believing in superpowers I didn't even know I had.

Acknowledgments

I must acknowledge my King, Jesus the Christ, and the Holy Spirit, for guiding and encouraging me all the way from start to finish. Thank you to Nadia Adams, who helped with typing when my vision became so poor I could barely see, and to Margaret Hiltz, the encouraging voice from beginning to end. I also want to thank the many friends, residents, and employees at All Seasons. Your support meant more than words can say.

Angels do exist on this earth. I would like to thank Dr. Jasmine Zapata and Coach Julia of Motivational M.D. Publishing for their consistent encouragement and help.

FOREWORD

On October 30, 1944, in a small town in Florida, a pugilist was born. Raised as an only child, she beat the odds of a convoluted and tumultuous childhood and came to understand the importance of *carpe diem* and self-resilience through her faith in God.

She emerged from the Civil Rights era as a mother of three boys. Soon after, she gave birth to me, the only female to inherit her genes, DNA, and resilience to pursue motivational, spiritual, and emotional alignment with oneself.

Then came the last son she would give birth to, the result of an interracial marriage that consummated her family and created the most kaleidoscopic petri dish possible.

I have observed Joy over the past 54 years with immense tenacity, fortitude, and resilience. She has contributed tirelessly by pouring into people, children, marriages, churches, and institutions, nurturing and leaving a significant impact on every life she touched. There are hundreds of children she has taught and raised, not just the five she gave life to or the many she fostered.

Surely, cognitively and spiritually, she has lived up to her name. She has done just that, politely transforming into a conduit of all things good and godly, always stepping aside so that God could have the glory through her life and her work, which has undoubtedly faced an unfair and overwhelming number of challenges.

After her first bout with cancer, and then a second round, she was stricken with the rare skin disease vitiligo. Though the cancer attacks did not kill her, the intrusive effects of vitiligo and its cascading implications could have mentally annihilated her.

Instead, she used her ailment to solve new problems. She became a spokesperson for vitiligo to empower, inform, and encourage further research on the rare disease, creating true value from what once felt like a curse.

It was not until the third bout with cancer, at the seasoned age of 79, that I began to worry. We were in the closing rounds of the match with life. I feared the pugilist had seen her day and that all her limits had been pushed to the brink of collapse.

Yet again, she prevailed, as only Joy would.

Now I know she is not just a pugilist. She is the CHAMPION.

I am blessed to be her prodigy.

Vanessa Toliver

Introduction

Welcome to *The Transformation Café*, and thank you for taking the time to read this book. My name is Joy Croel, and I want to share a few things about myself.

I celebrated my 80th birthday shortly before the publishing of this book. I have raised four wonderful sons and a wonderful daughter. Many great children have also been a part of my extended family. After twelve years in my second marriage, we got divorced. I went on to college and earned an associate's degree in education. I then continued on to complete my bachelor's and master's degrees.

As a child, I never felt loved. I didn't know what that was like. My dad was an absent parent, but he was a great preacher. Although I learned a lot about the Bible from him and the church that my mom and the rest of my family attended, I did not fully believe the scriptures applied to me. Even though I learned the stories and believed they were true for others, I did not believe they were meant for me.

Having had a very abusive mother and never experiencing love as I do now, it was hard for me to conceive that a perfect God could love me.

But I made a decision to commit, and the more I read and learned about how much God truly did love me, I gradually began to believe that maybe, just maybe, it could be true for me.

After listening to many great preachers and teachers over the years, one day I walked into the living room where my husband was putting the kids' toys together for Christmas. I looked into the eyes of a man who truly loved me. It felt as if, for the very first time, I experienced the kind of love I had never believed could apply to me.

I immediately went upstairs, got my Bible, and began to read it. I read it as though it was written by someone who loved me and wanted me to have that information.

> **I read it as though it was written by someone who loved me and wanted me to have that information. I began to believe what the Bible said.**

I began to believe what the Bible said and started applying the things I learned from reading it. I began in Genesis, the beginning of the Bible, and discovered where I came from and that my life truly does have value. I share some of the things that impacted my life in those early days because I've learned that sometimes it helps to take small steps in the process, rather than trying to change everything at once.

I wrote *The Transformation Cafe* for the person who is looking for real answers and tools to change their thinking, attitude, and life situations so they can become all that God has designed them to be. Reading this book will begin a life-changing journey for you because within it, you will find keys that unlock many of the questions you may have.

Introduction

This book is briefly about my journey. Even though it felt like, at times, I was only eating crumbs, I was still sharing the Word of God with many people. I even became ordained at one point. Still, it took years to believe that those great promises could truly belong to me. Today, I am so blessed. I am a changed person, and I hope you will experience the same transformation in your life.

As you read this book, think of it like a cafe — hence the name, *The Transformation Cafe*. When you go to a restaurant, the first thing they do is hand you the menu and bring you water and maybe some bread, especially if you're in the right kind of restaurant. You then choose your entree, your salad, and your main meal.

Sometimes, you go into a restaurant and don't have time to enjoy a full meal. You might have a small drink, a salad, or a light entree. Other times, you're ready for a full four-course meal. That's how *The Transformation Cafe* works. I share bits and pieces you can nibble on and think about throughout the day. There are other times when you might need a full-course meal and have time to read longer passages of scripture, full books, or chapters. Sometimes you may need a lot of information because you're in a season that requires deep support. Other times, you just need a word from the Lord.

You will find that you can come back and look at these notes again and again to get the nourishment you need. I remember moving into my current apartment and finding some notes I had written in a notebook about ten years earlier. As I read them, I thought, "Oh yeah, that's what God told me. That's what I was thinking. That makes sense to me now."

This book will be like a buffet for you to enjoy. There may be times when you sit down and study for 30 minutes, an hour, or even a whole evening to research and meditate. And there will be other times when all you have time for is a verse or two — like taking a quick sip of tea or a warm cup of cocoa.

The strategies I'm going to share with you throughout this book will sometimes feel like a tall glass of lemonade or water. They will be refreshing thoughts for you to consume, and then you'll be on your way.

But there will also be times when I share deeper insights and tools I have found in the Bible — things that make life easier, better, or simply more interesting. These are the moments that will settle in and nourish you the way a full meal would. These are the things I encourage you to write down in your notebook and meditate on.

It can be a simple spiral notebook or a journal where you write down your questions and the answers you receive. You can use it to keep track of prayers you've prayed and the answers to those prayers. This is important, because the enemy will try to steal that information from you and distract you from keeping track of your progress.

God has a plan and a purpose for each of us, so let's move forward together, believing in a God who truly loves us and can transform us from who we presently are to who we were created to be.

Chapter 1

Understand the Real Questions

Life is full of real questions that deserve real answers. It is important to answer the questions in life that are essential to your success. In this chapter, we will begin to explore how to recognize and hear those real questions. This chapter will help you reflect on them as you begin moving toward the greatness that is within you.

To fully understand where you've come from helps you set clear goals for where you want to go. This is why it's so important to recognize the right questions in life. Doing so empowers you to move in new circles, set meaningful goals, and achieve them.

The danger of not knowing where you've come from is that you may spend time and energy answering the wrong questions, or giving responses to things that were never asked. You may even give misleading answers you never intended to give.

> **To fully understand where you've come from, helps you set goals as to where you want to go.**

There was a little boy around six or seven years old who came running into the house to find his mom busy cleaning in the kitchen. The boy had a questioning look on his face and asked, "Mom, where did I come from?"

His mother, who had long awaited this question, got a hot cup of coffee, sat down at the table, took a deep breath, and began to explain the story of reproduction and childbirth. When she finally finished, she looked at her son and asked if he had any questions. He just smiled and said, "James said he came from Cleveland, and I was just wondering where I came from."

The mother in this story answered according to her perception of what her son was asking. However, it was not the real question her son had. This reminds us how important it is to truly understand the questions being asked — especially the ones that are essential to your growth and success.

Are you struggling with where you are right now? Are you frustrated with the present circumstances in your life that led you to this point? Your answers to these important questions will shape the thoughts that lead to the actions you take moving forward.

As you begin to understand where you've come from and identify when and where you've made certain decisions, it will help you make better decisions in the future. You must quiet the questions that feed your doubts, anxiety, fear, anger, and suspicion. We also need to stop entertaining the false narratives we have received from others based on misinformation or past experiences.

Harv Eker says, "Don't believe anything you think." Getting honest with yourself and staying focused on the real questions will help you become the person you were created to be.

Here are 7 real questions you might need to be asking yourself. Fill in some of your thoughts below:

1. How did I get to this place where I currently am?

_____
_____
_____
_____
_____
_____

2. Do I perceive myself as physically attractive and healthy, or do I see myself as overweight or underweight? Why or why not? What is one small step I can take to change or improve this perception or reality?

_____
_____
_____
_____
_____
_____

3. Is there something you want to change about your appearance?

_____
_____
_____
_____
_____
_____

4. What has caused you to be stuck in a hole and want to get out?

_____
_____
_____
_____
_____
_____

5. Have you made the decision that you are comfortable where you are? How did you come to that decision?

_____
_____
_____
_____
_____
_____

6. What do you believe about yourself that allows you to stay in this situation?

_____
_____
_____
_____
_____
_____

7. What decisions did you make, good or bad that got you here?

_____
_____
_____
_____
_____
_____

Chapter 2
Know and Understand Your Purpose

Before you were born, you were a seed in the soil of your mother's womb. Over the years, as people poured into your life, your experiences have helped you develop into the person you are today. However, that may not be the person God intended you to be. Some of your experiences were good, and some were not so great. What often happens is that you begin to give meaning to those experiences and make judgments about yourself that may or may not be true. This is why it is so important to know and understand your purpose.

For example, if a fish attempted to climb a tree, it would be considered a failure because it does not understand its purpose. Another example is the negative statements you may have heard as a child, when you were not able to distinguish between truth and untruth. A statement like "bad boy" after breaking a toy may have led you to believe you were a bad person. Or if a teacher corrected a mistake on your paper, you may have started to believe you were not smart enough.

The reason it is so hard for many people to know and understand their purpose is because they misinterpret the information they receive throughout life.

Many of you may still be living your life according to those negative voices. It is like eating a bad piece of fruit, such as a peach, and deciding to hate peaches for the rest of your life. The problem with that is you miss the deliciousness of what peaches are meant to be. The only way to silence negative voices is to get new information from a source you trust. Then, you must choose to believe that new information and apply it to your life.

As a young woman, I met some very dynamic and successful female evangelists and preachers. I wanted so badly to go on the road and preach. I had already received several local invitations. However, I had three babies, each 18 months apart in age, and my mother was not about to babysit all those babies. My husband, who was working full time, said, "Stay home." My pastor said that my kids were my first congregation. So I stayed home and fed my kids the "food" from what would later become *The Transformation Cafe*, because I understood my purpose at that time. I was later able to travel as my children got older.

> **The only way to silence negative voices is to get new information that comes from a source you consider valid. You then must choose to believe the new information and apply it to your life.**

Know and Understand Your Purpose

There may be times when you have been encouraged to do things that you are in no way equipped to do, or it may simply not be the right time or place. For example, you could try using a cellphone to remove snow from your driveway in the winter, especially if you live in Michigan, but that is not the purpose it was designed for. It would take much longer and be far more difficult. This is why knowing and understanding your purpose is so important.

Many Christians, as well as non-Christians, do not experience the joy that could be theirs because their lives are not aligned with God's word. Some do not trust God, and others simply do not know what His word says.

As you explore your purpose through prayer and study, your Heavenly Father will begin to give you clarity and insight. Also, be sure to ask God if this is the right time for you. Remember, a "no" may not be permanent. It may simply mean "**Not Now**" or "not with this person."

Here are 3 action steps you can take to begin the journey of knowing and understanding your purpose:

1. Prayerfully seek the wisdom of God
2. Ask God to open your eyes as to what problem you were created to solve
3. Seek the wisdom of your leaders, but remember always to use the priority of God's wisdom

Discussion Questions

1. What Am I extremely passionate about?
   _____
   _____
   _____
   _____
   _____

2. What am I often praised or complimented for?
   _____
   _____
   _____
   _____
   _____

3. What do I enjoy doing most of all?
   _____
   _____
   _____
   _____
   _____

Chapter 3
Learn to Believe In and Love Yourself

In this chapter of *The Transformation Cafe*, we get into some meat and potatoes. This is what I mean when I say learn to believe in and love yourself. When you love something, you take care of it. When you believe in yourself, your actions begin to change. You will do things differently than you would if you didn't believe in yourself. When you believe in and love yourself, you take better care of yourself. Learning to believe in and love yourself means that you value yourself.

I know what it's like not to love or believe in yourself. I struggled most of my life with self-doubt. I used to think of my life as a dump pile. But over many years of learning, forgetting what I learned, and having to learn it all over again, things began to change. I remember a time when I felt very ugly and would seldom look in the mirror. I had a tooth in the front of my mouth that was coming loose. Because it was hanging down, I started thinking about ways to get it fixed.

It wasn't long before a pastor visited our congregation, and we started talking about my tooth. He asked why I hadn't gotten it fixed. I told him I didn't have very much money, and he said,

"No problem. I work at the dental school, and I'll fix it for you at no cost." I couldn't believe how gorgeous I looked after that tooth was fixed. From that moment on, I began to take better care of myself — my kids, my house, and even my car.

But most of all, I worked on my mind and my thought process. I read books like *Awaken the Giant Within* by Tony Robbins and *Think and Grow Rich* by Napoleon Hill. I had to read that one three times. Now I read it every year, along with my Bible daily. I also read other books by great teachers over the years. I gradually learned to love myself by getting new information and by appreciating who God made me to be.

I began to think, if God loved me, then it must be okay for me to love myself and be kinder to myself. That led me to start treating myself better, little by little. I never gave up on myself, and it is important that you don't give up on yourself either.

As you continue to read good books, study, believe, and apply what you learn, along with applying the Bible to your life, you will begin to feel better and think more positively about yourself. You will become more aware of the good things in your life and start accepting them.

I eventually stopped thinking of my life as a dump pile and started to believe that I was made in the image of God, and that I had real value. I wish I had the strategies from *The Transformation Cafe* back then as I was going through those years, but I am so glad to be able to share them with you now.

I believe the 7 strategies listed below will help you grow much faster than I did and avoid much of the pain along the way.

Learn to Believe In and Love Yourself

1. Begin telling yourself that your life has value.
2. Believe that you are destined for greatness.
3. Believe that God loves you more than you could ever love yourself.
4. Read the Bible daily for wisdom and direction in life.
5. Join a Bible study, either online or at your local church if available.
6. Ask a trusted friend what church they attend, and go visit with them.
7. Memorize the names of the first five books of the Bible.

Chapter 4
Seek the One Resource That Will Change Your Life

There are many resources people look to in order to make the changes they want in their lives, but most of these are short-lived and offer little long-term effectiveness. We watch commercials on television and find that every few minutes someone is selling something to create a solution to our problems. There is a beauty cream for every skincare flaw and all kinds of chemicals for health problems. If you're lonely, there is a commercial for that. If you feel too fat or too skinny, there is a commercial for that too. But in the end, they rarely provide the lasting value you are seeking.

Having an alcoholic mother while growing up impacted my life very deeply. It made me feel like my life had no value, like it wasn't worth living. I had no concept of "me" at all. Like many people, I tried everything I thought would make a difference in my life. At the age of nine, I just shut down. I used to run across the main street in my hometown in front of traffic to see if the cars would hit me or stop.

Then one day, it dawned on me that it didn't make sense to live in hell and then die and go to hell too. The church I went to taught that if I committed suicide, I would go to hell. I kept trying anything that would help make a permanent change in my behavior, but the results were always temporary. When the next day or the next week came, the problem was still there.

But even at that young age, I loved reading the stories in the Bible and learning about places and people — and most of all, learning about God. It was at the age of nine that I began to seek the one resource that would change my life permanently.

If you are searching for real transformation in your life, there is one resource I can recommend that truly has the ability to help you change your life permanently. Understand this: You have access to the Creator of the Universe, and that is a resource even better than Google. When you need help or information, I encourage you to go to the Highest Source possible. Accessing God is just a prayer away, and it can be done anywhere and at any time.

You can download any number of Bible translations on your phone. God has also given you His Holy Spirit as a guide to help you along the way. No special tools are needed. There are books, recordings, and preachers everywhere. Ask your friends or another church member for referrals.

I have learned to listen for and recognize the voice of God, and I believe that if you seek God, He will find you. He is not the one who is lost.

Seek the One Resource That Will Change Your Life

> **I've learned to listen and recognize the voice of God. I believe if you seek God He will find you.
> He is not the one lost.**

There was once a man who saved up every penny he could for a ship's passage to America. When he bought his ticket, he did not realize that meals were included in the fare. He ate crumbs and leftovers from the kitchen. So often, we miss out because we do not understand what comes with being a child of God.

No, God is not Father Christmas, nor does He carry a magic wand ready to grant your every wish. God is a loving Father who cares deeply for you and desires the very best for your life.

One evening, I was upstairs in our apartment and heard a noise downstairs. I looked around and realized my husband was not in bed with me. I rolled out of bed, crept downstairs, and peeked around the corner. There he was, putting the children's toys together. He looked up at me, and for the first time in my life, I looked into the eyes of someone whom I believed truly loved me.

I thought, if this man could love me with his pea-sized brain, what must the love of God be like?

You see, I had heard about the love of God all my life. My father was a preacher, and I had read the Bible for as long as I could remember. I studied it regularly, yet I never truly believed that God loved me; that the promises I read about were actually for me.

It is absolutely possible for you to experience real transformation. But in order to change your behaviour, you must first change your attitude. And to change your attitude, you need new information — information from a source you consider trustworthy. For me, that source is the Holy Bible.

I want to encourage you to seek out the one resource that, when applied, will change your life. The Bible says in Romans 12:2 (KJV): "And be not conformed to this world: but be ye transformed by the renewing of your mind, that ye may prove what is that good, and acceptable, and perfect, will of God."

> "And be not conformed to this world: but be ye **transformed by the renewing of your mind,** that ye may prove what is that good, and acceptable, and perfect, will of God."
> Romans 12:2 (KJV)

Here are 4 practices that will help you on your journey of seeking the one resource that will change your life.

1. Ask God to lead you and trust that He will do it.
2. Keep a journal of things that have stood out in your mind, even if it's only a few sentences.
3. Memorize 1-3 verses in the bible that have special meaning to you.
4. Seek out a bible study to become a part of.

As a child of God, I have been so blessed in every area of my life, and I want the same for you. We sometimes do not know or realize that we have access to the mind of God and the Holy Spirit as a guide to help us. No, my life has not been perfect, and I have made some foolish mistakes along the way, but God has been there as I have learned to listen for and recognize His voice.

REFLECTIONS

1. What in your bible reading today stood out in your mind?

_____
_____
_____
_____
_____
_____

2. Will you post a comment on my Facebook page about what you have learnt this week concerning your relationship with God and how it has affected your relationship with others?
Here is the link: https://m.facebook.com/thetransformationcafe/.

Chapter 5

Understand, There's a Manual For This!

Isn't it funny how some people, when they have a project to put together that requires reading the manual, will only read it after spending countless hours trying to assemble it on their own, often ending up with a bag of screws left over? **Don't do that.**

Did you know that life comes with a manual? Yes, there really is a manual to help you understand how to go from where you are to where God designed you to be. But you have to read it, and that manual is the Bible.

2 Timothy 3:16–17 (KJV) says: *"All scripture is given by inspiration of God, and is profitable for doctrine, for reproof, for correction, for instruction in righteousness: That the man of God may be perfect, thoroughly furnished unto all good works."*

So why is this important? So that the man or woman of God will be complete, trained, and made ready for every good work. If you're looking for a success manual, the Bible is the success book of all ages. It was written by the One who created you.

In Psalm 119:105, it says: *"Thy word is a lamp unto my feet, and a light unto my path."* If you don't want to stumble through life, falling into every pothole along the way, the Bible is the book to study.

It is also very important to become familiar with the books of the Bible. The Bible is not just one book, but 66 different books and letters. It's like a buffet filled with all kinds of interesting and nourishing information to feed your spirit.

This topic is close to me because there was a time in my life when I did not understand who I was, and I did not recognize my true value. I had been a Bible teacher since I was 16 years old, but I eventually began to realize that I was not really applying the Bible to my own life.

Over the years, however, things began to change. I began to think of Jesus as He is described in the scriptures. The more I read and studied, the more the Word became real to me.

Some of the things I did in the beginning were:

- I **chose** to believe the bible.
- I **chose** to apply what I understood.
- I **began** to journal in my notebook.

I read the Bible as though it was written by somebody who loved me and wanted me to have this information. I chose to believe it, and my life has not been the same since. It was as though I had found the key to the food pantry, and I could feast as much as I wanted.

Understand, There's a Manual For This!

Here are some suggestions to help you on your journey of being transformed from who you presently are to who you were created to be, as you study the Bible:

1. Understand the difference between the Old Testament and the New Testament.
   The Old Testament points us to Christ by giving us the history of God's people. The New Testament reveals the life of Christ and His sacrifice, along with the benefits He provides for us as God's children.

2. Think about what the Bible says in the following verses, and try to memorize at least one of them:
   a. 2 Kings 20:5 (NIV) reminds you that delay does not mean denial. *"... I have heard your prayer and seen your tears; I will heal you.*
   b. 2 Thessalonians 3:3 (NIV) reminds you of God's faithfulness to strengthen and protect you. *"But the Lord is faithful, and The Lord will strengthen you and protect you from the evil one."*

3. Other scriptures to look up and meditate on.
   a. When you are **lonely**, read Hebrews 13:5
   b. When you are **anxious**, read Psalms 23:1-6
   c. When you are **angry**, read Ephesians 4:26
   d. When you are **afraid**, read Isaiah 41:10
   e. When you are **confused**, read Proverbs 3:5-6
   f. When you are **in doubt**, read Proverbs 1:1-7

Chapter 6

Find Your Support Group

No Christian has ever been called to "go it alone" in his or her walk of faith. This is why it is so important that you find your tribe.

The Bible says in Hebrews 10:24–25 (NIV): *"Let us consider one another in order to stir up love and good works, not forsaking the assembling of ourselves together, as is the manner of some, but exhorting one another — and so much the more as you see the Day approaching."*

Perhaps you've heard someone say, "Oh, I don't go to church very often. I'd rather stay at home and watch sermons on television." Or maybe, "I downloaded a podcast from my favorite preacher." You may have also heard, "I go online and listen to a preacher or teacher," or, "I only go to church when I can work it into my family's schedule." Sometimes people say, "I go as often as I can," which usually means not often at all.

> **It is very important to have people that help in your spiritual growth and development, and that nurture you as you develop and grow into the person God designed you to become.**

There are many reasons people give for not attending church. Some refuse to join because they may have had a terrible experience with religious people. Others live so far from a biblically sound fellowship that they feel it isn't feasible for them to be active members. Some people are shy and find it difficult to open up to others. Others object to the hypocrisy they perceive in organized congregations. And then there are those who are so afraid of being rejected that they isolate themselves from others, including other Christians.

I was abused as a child. I grew up thinking that people wanted to hurt me. But I eventually learned to trust God to keep me safe and to give me friends and family who would help me grow, and allow me to help others grow as well.

I remember, as a young woman, attending a church shortly after I got married. The congregation was small, and most of the members were older. As I attended Sunday School, my knowledge of the scriptures became clear very quickly. It wasn't long before I was asked to teach Sunday School. The congregation grew rapidly.

In another church I attended later in life, I heard from members that the pastor often quoted me during his comments. Although he never said anything directly to me, he always spoke very highly of my understanding of the scriptures. That

Find Your Support Group

blessed me deeply, and my confidence in what God had taught me continued to grow.

These two congregations were a wonderful support system. They helped me speak up and share what I had learned with more confidence, which encouraged me to study even more.

It is very important to have people who support your spiritual growth and development, and who nurture you as you grow into the person God designed you to be. Having people to study with and share your faith journey will strengthen both your knowledge and your faith.

Here are 4 important things you can do that will help you in your growth and development.

1. Give yourself 1 new friend in the church community each month.
2. Commit to at least 1 service a week and be as consistent as possible.
3. Spend 30-45 minutes a week in bible study.
4. Memorize 1 chapter in the Bible a week

Chapter 7

Look for the Well

In this chapter, let me share one last story with you, found in Genesis chapter 21, starting at verse 8. But please read the entire chapter so you can gain a full understanding of what happened between three people and God.

In Bible days, they did not have running water in homes like we do today. There was usually a well in some area of the community where women would go to draw water for use in their homes. Wells, rivers, streams, lakes, or oceans were the only sources of water supply for the communities in those days. They contained water, the life source for the people. It was also a place where women gathered to share information and, at times, the latest gossip.

But let's focus on the simple fact that a well is a hole in the ground that contains water. In this story, a young woman was in the desert, and she had no water. Water is absolutely vital for life and a key component of all living organisms. This young woman was in the desert with her child, and they had no water.

God opened her eyes to see His provision — a well nearby.

The well represents God's resources. His provision has done that for me many times when I've found myself in a difficult place, often a situation of my own making. I didn't know what to do, and I didn't know how to do it. Then I prayed to God, "Show me your resources. Show me what you have for me in this situation. Show me how." And the resources would soon become apparent in my life. Somehow, they would come. I would receive the information I needed.

> **"But my God shall supply all your need according to His riches in glory by Christ Jesus."**
> **Philippians 4:19 (KJV)**

On more than one occasion, God has provided the resources I needed during a desperate situation. One morning, when the boys were very young, they were having breakfast, and the youngest one dropped the milk jar on the floor. It shattered, and milk and glass went everywhere. I shouted, "Oh my God, that was the last of the milk." I sent the boys and my daughter off to school, cleaned up the mess, and set out to find not only milk but other food as well. Not only was that the last of the milk, it was also the last of the food in the house. And did I forget to mention? I had no money either.

I went to all the food banks and every place I knew that gave out food, but I had no luck at all. By the time the kids were due home, I pulled into the park near my house, parked, and prayed Psalm 37:25: *"I was young and now I am old, yet I have never seen the righteous forsaken nor his seed begging bread."* I just hung my head. I didn't know how God was going to fix it. I only knew that I had nowhere else to turn. I pulled into the driveway and went into the house. The kitchen was full of food. The counters were covered. The refrigerator, freezer, and table were packed. There was even a box of canned goods on the floor.

All I could say was, "Thank you, God."

Another time, I received an eviction notice. They were scheduled to come the next day to set my things out on the street. Then, one of the places I applied to, which told me there was a two-year waiting list, called and said I could come pick up my keys that very day.

All I could say was, "Thank you, Lord."

Here is a helpful strategy for finding your well, God's resources, and how you can access it: **Pray and ask God to open your eyes so you can see His provision.** The well may be a meeting you need to attend. It may be a neighbor or a child who needs your help, or a phone call you need to make. As we come to the close of this book, the most important takeaway I want to leave with you is this: God will always provide what you need. Remember, Jesus died so that you could have life, and have it more abundantly. (John 10:10)

LOOK FOR THE WELL, RECEIVE GOD'S RESOURCES, ...AND BE TRANSFORMED.

Closing Reflections

Thank you for dining at The Transformation Cafe. I hope this book has been a blessing and a help in your walk with the Lord and the Word of God.

God bless and keep you.

Joy Croel

About the Author

Joy Croel was an only child, born to a very beautiful and extremely talented, yet alcoholic mother with serious issues. At age 15, Joy married a 17-year-old soldier. Three years later, she had her first son. Eighteen months after that, her second son was born. Then, you guessed it, eighteen months later came her third son. It was just a house full of kids.

Five years later, Joy finally had her only daughter, and five years after that, another son. All she knew about being an adult was what she saw on television.

After her second marriage and divorce, Joy went to college and, in just 16 months, earned her associate's degree in education. She continued on to earn her master's degree from Cambridge College and has served in many roles in the field of education, including teacher, principal, and consultant.

In the meantime, she began teaching her students the things she knew they needed to succeed in life. She created a financial literacy program that enriched the lives of over 300 students, teaching practical life skills alongside their regular curriculum.

Joy became a licensed, ordained evangelist after teaching and preaching the Word of God since the age of 16. She also hosted her own television program for more than seven years, produced three radio programs, and attended seminary for a short time, all while raising five children.

After beating cancer three times, she finally decided it was time to retire. Over the years, Joy explored a variety of occupations and eventually found her niche in sales, along with teaching and sharing the Word of God. She combined her love of scripture with her passion for education to inspire others.

For more information on bulk purchases or speaking events, please contact the author at: JoyCroel@gmail.com or visit https://www.facebook.com/thetransformationcafe.

Notes

Notes

Notes

Notes

Notes

Notes

Notes

Notes

Notes

Notes

Made in the USA
Columbia, SC
06 June 2025